Pick up a pencil and get writing — with CGP!

The best way for pupils to improve their handwriting skills in Reception (ages 4-5) is by doing as much practice as they can.

That's where this book comes in. It's packed with activities to help them get off to a flying start in their writing careers.

And as you'd expect from CGP, everything's presented in a friendly and colourful style to make learning to write as much fun as possible!

What CGP is all about

Our sole aim here at CGP is to produce the highest quality books — carefully written, immaculately presented and dangerously close to being funny.

Then we work our socks off to get them out to you — at the cheapest possible prices.

Handwriting Hints

1. Sit up straight at your desk or at a table.

2. Use a pencil to trace the lines, letters and numbers. You can use coloured pencils to colour in the pictures.

3. Get a grown-up to help you hold your pencil properly. Use your right or left hand — whichever you find easier.

4. If you find a letter tricky, try tracing it in the air or on a piece of paper with your finger. Then do it with the pencil.

5. Work neatly. Try and keep your pencil on top of the dotty lines or inside the lines.

Hints for Helpers

Here are a few things to bear in mind when using this book:
- Every school has its own handwriting style. Some schools may form letters differently to how they're written here — for example, k instead of k. Check with the school to see how they write each letter.
- In this book, some of the letters have flicks at the bottom in preparation for joined-up writing. Again, check to see how these letters are written in school.
- For each letter, there is a red dot showing where to start, and arrows to follow to complete the letter. Some of the lines on the first few pages also have starting dots.
- The book should be worked through in order — it gets harder as you go through, and builds on content covered earlier in the book.
- You can help by reading the instructions out loud, and by sounding out the letters and words on the pages.

Contents

Straight Lines 2

Wavy Lines 3

Loops 4

Zigzag and Boxy Lines 5

Shapes at the Circus 6

Shapes at the Beach 7

c, o and a 8

i, l and t 9

u, y and j 10

r, n and m 11

h and k 12

b and p 13

d, g and q 14

e, s and f 15

v, w, x and z 16

The Alphabet 17

Numbers 20

Grand Finale 22

Published by CGP

Editors: Chris Corrall, Joanna Daniels, Caley Simpson
Reviewer: Anne James
With thanks to Karen Wells for the proofreading.
ISBN: 978 1 78294 694 6

Clipart from Corel®
Printed by Elanders Ltd, Newcastle upon Tyne.
Based on the classic CGP style created by Richard Parsons.

Text, design, layout and original illustrations © Coordination Group Publications Ltd. (CGP) 2016
All rights reserved.

**Photocopying this book is not permitted, even if you have a CLA licence.
Extra copies are available from CGP with next day delivery • 0800 1712 712 • www.cgpbooks.co.uk**

Straight Lines

Trace the paths of these shooting stars! Start at the red dots. Then colour in the wizard.

Start at the red dots and draw over the dotted lines to finish off the ladders.

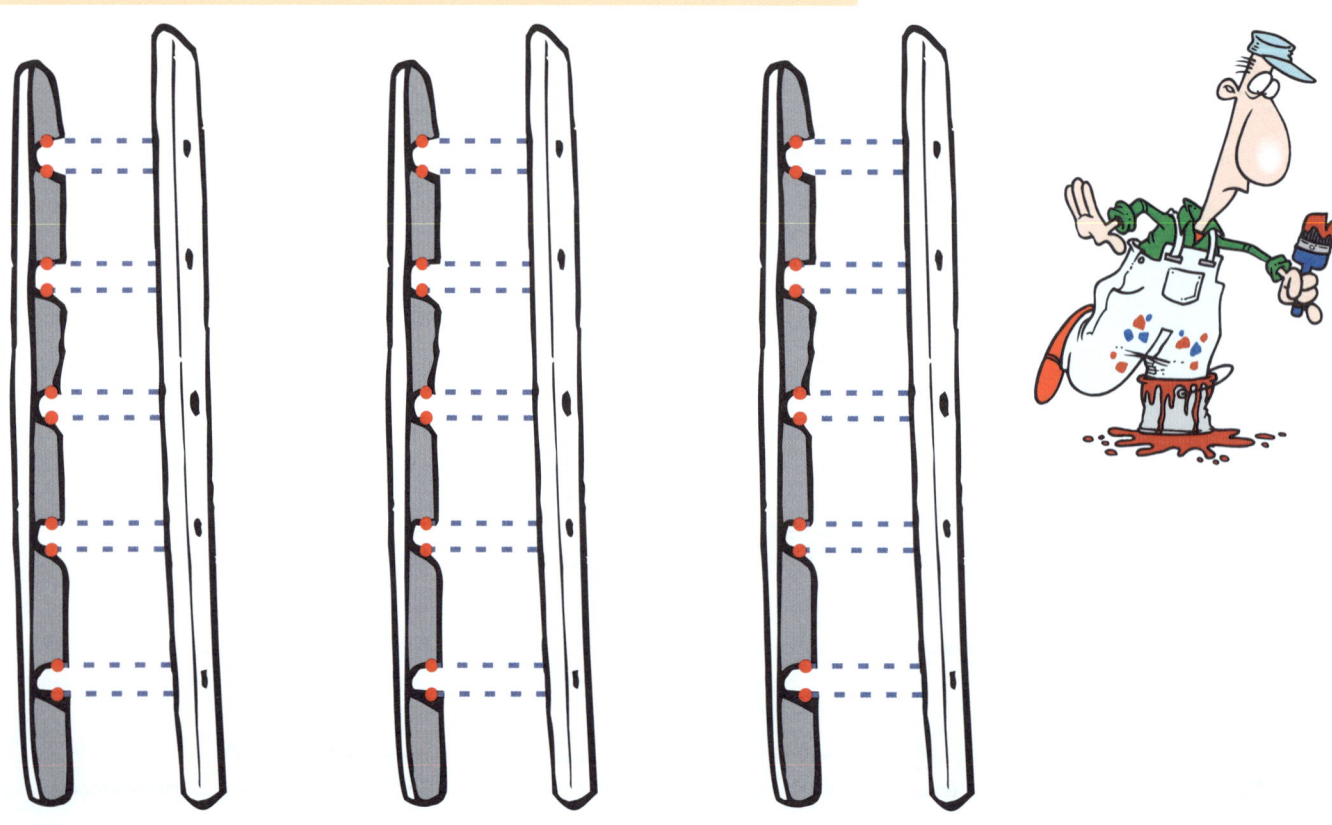

Wavy Lines

Start at the red dots and trace over these wavy lines. When you've finished, colour in the worm.

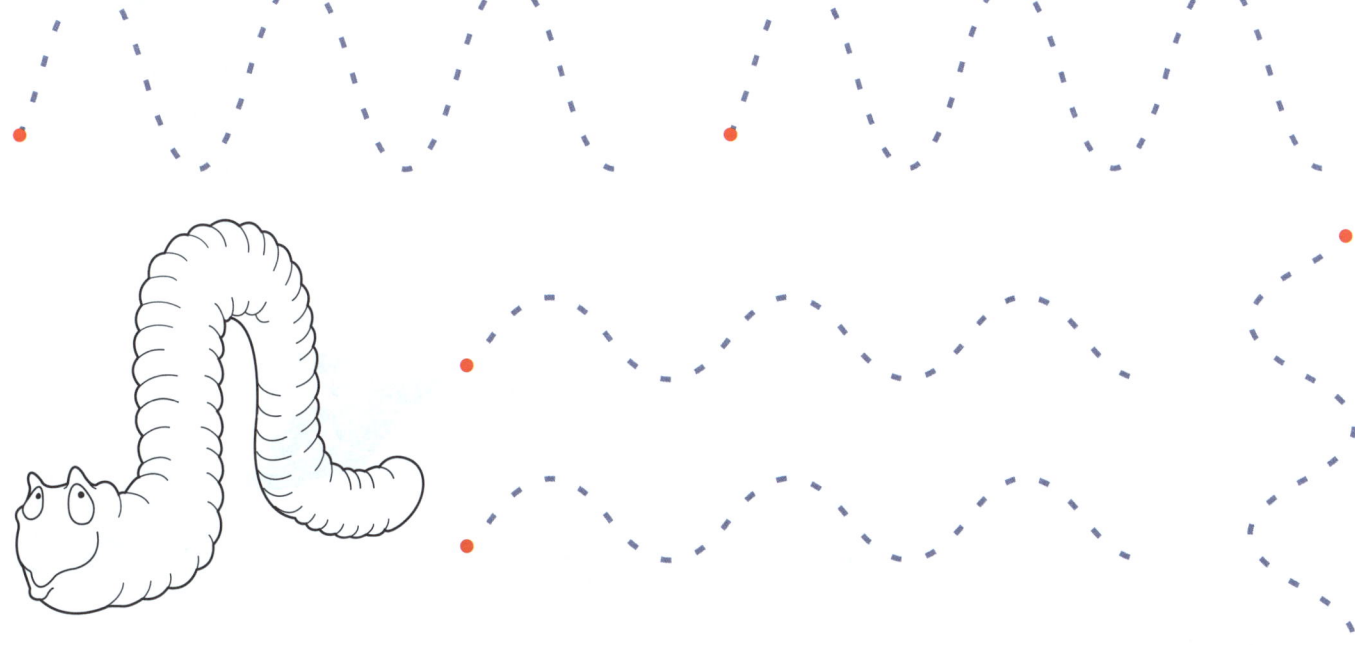

Draw around the trees, then colour them in.

Loops

Trace the loops behind the planes.
Start with your pencil on the red dots.

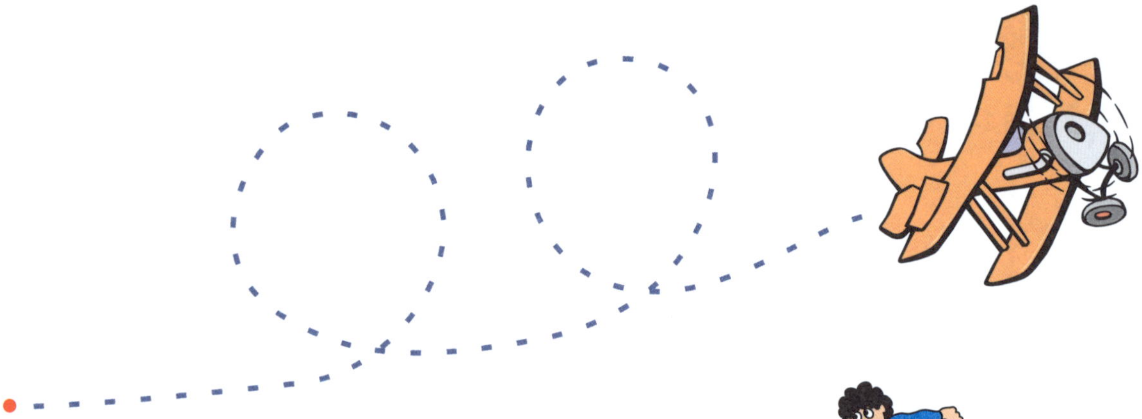

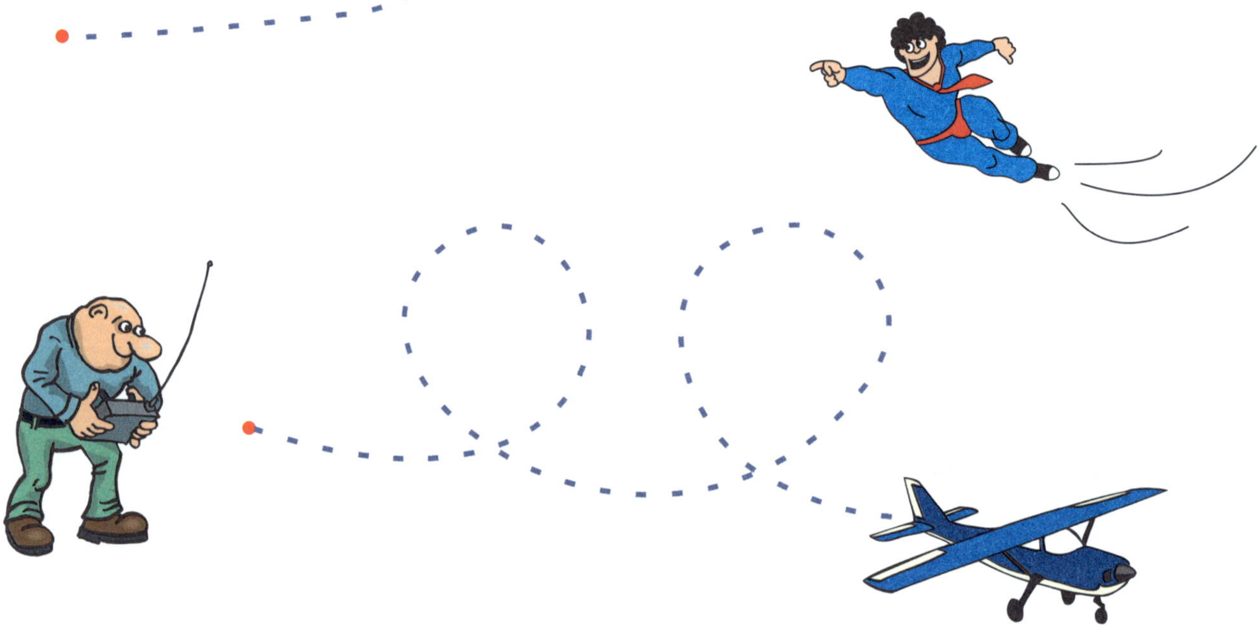

Zigzag and Boxy Lines

Trace these zigzags. Then colour in the dinosaur. Remember to start with your pencil on the red dots.

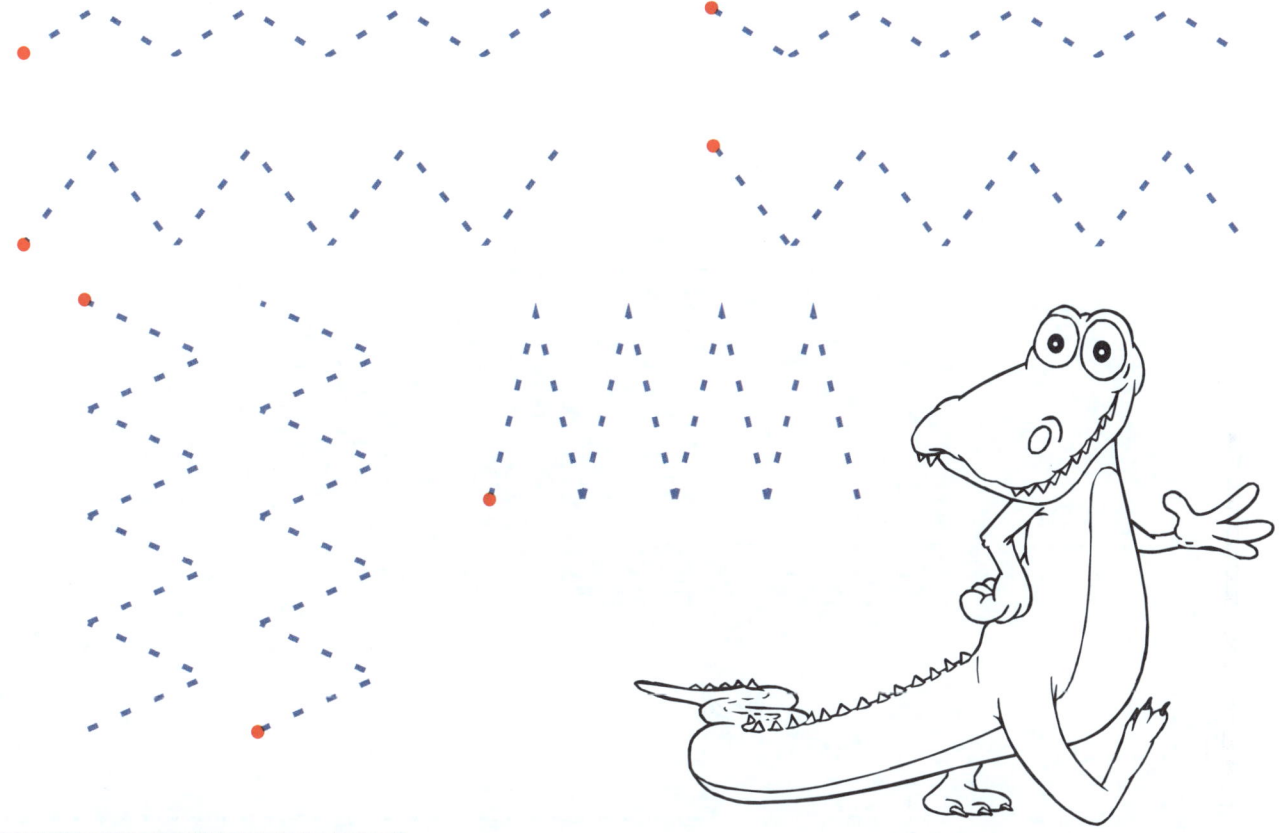

Finish off the castle!

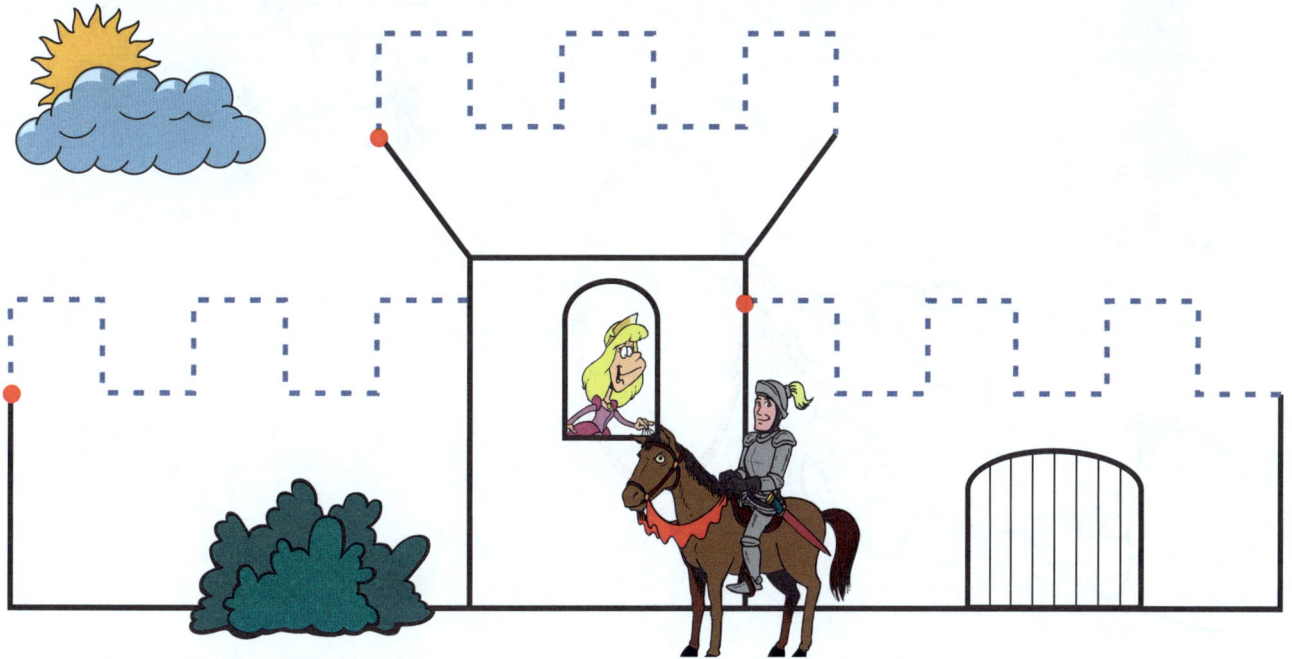

Shapes at the Circus

Trace over the dotty lines to bring the circus to life! Then colour in all the pictures.

Shapes at the Beach

Draw over the dotty lines to finish off the beach.
Don't forget to colour it in when you're done!

c, o and a

Draw over the dotty lines to trace these letters. Start at the red dots and follow the arrows.

Can you trace these letters and stay inside the lines? Colour in the pictures when you've finished.

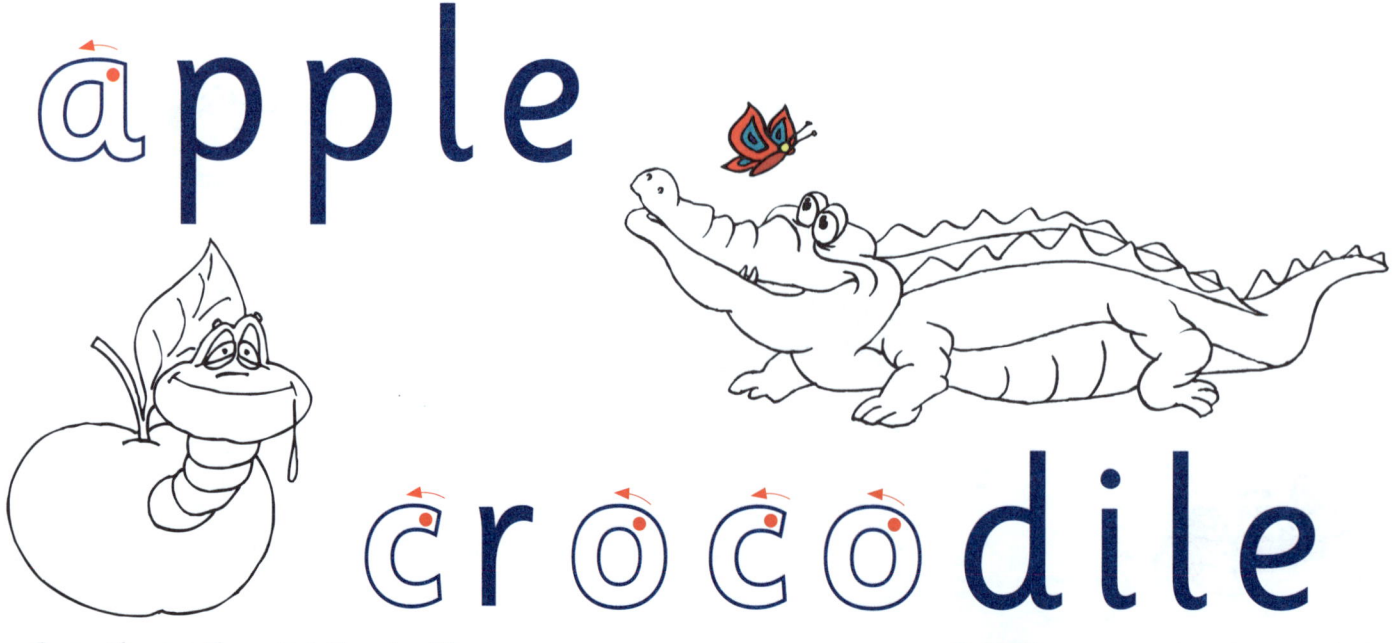

i, l and t

These letters all start with a straight line then have a flick. Follow the dotty lines to trace them.

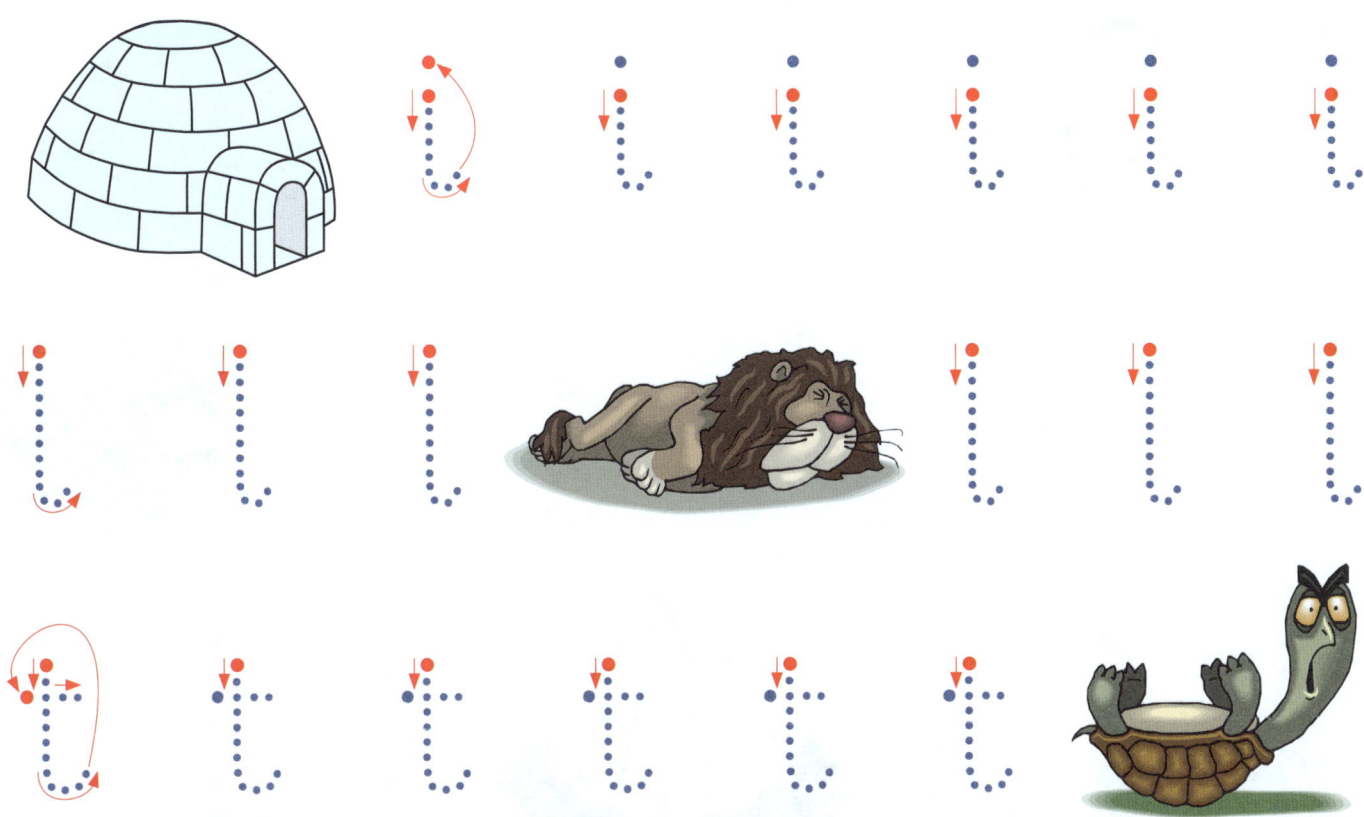

Trace the missing letters to finish these words. Then colour in the train and the snail.

u, y and j

Start at the red dots and draw over the dotty lines. Use the arrows to help you.

u  u u u u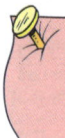

y y y y y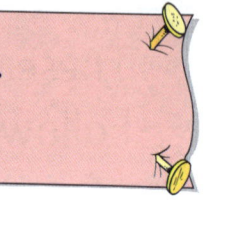

j j j  j j j

Trace these letters and stay inside the lines. When you've traced the letters, there are two pictures to colour in.

juggle
bunny

r, n and m

Start at the red dots and draw down then back up again. Then follow the rest of the dotty lines to finish the letters.

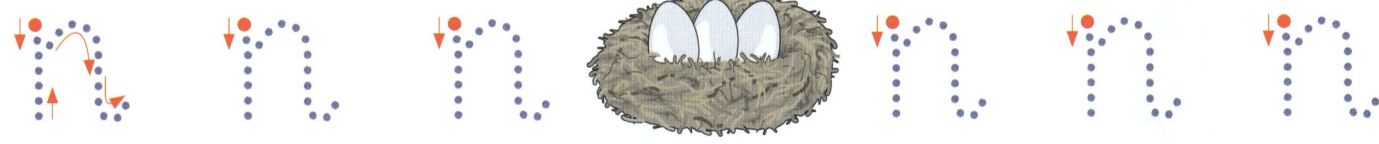

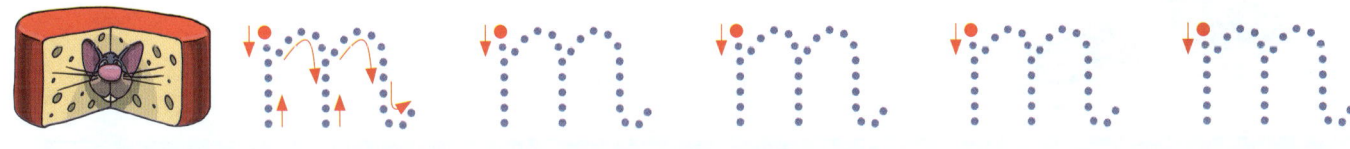

Start at the red dots and trace the letters. Make sure you stay inside the lines. Once you've finished, colour in the pictures.

monkey

frog

h and k

Now try these two letters. Trace carefully over the dotty lines, following the red arrows.

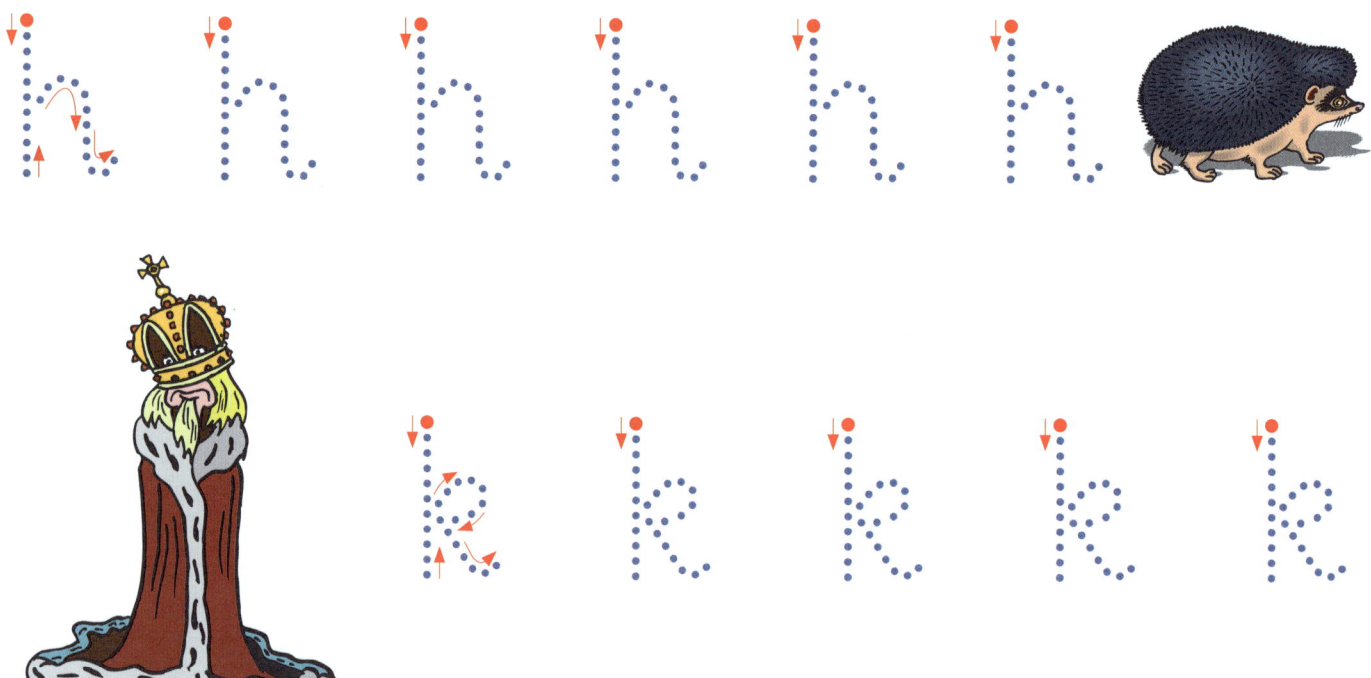

These words have some letters missing. Trace the letters and stay inside the lines. Then you can colour in the pictures.

Reception — Targeted Handwriting © CGP — not to be photocopied

b and p

These letters have a straight line and then a loop.
Follow the arrows around the dotty lines to trace them.

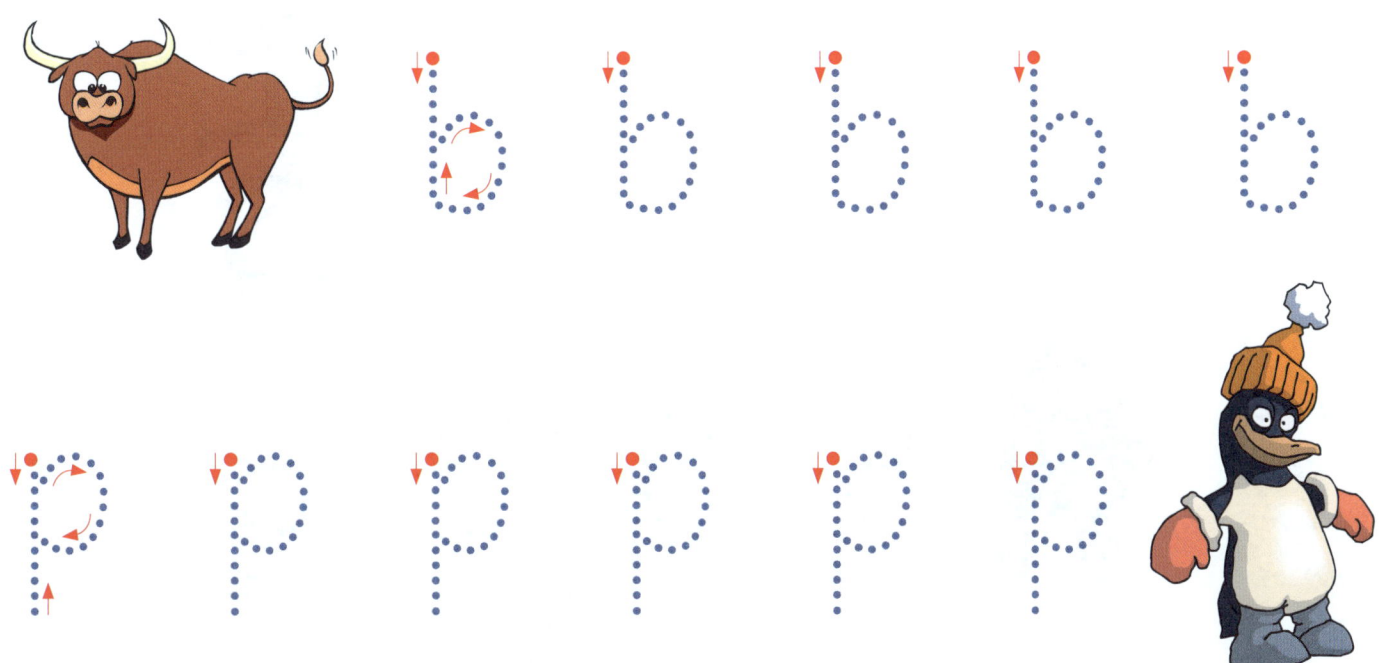

Now trace these letters and stay inside the lines.
There are some pictures to colour in when you've finished.

d, g and q

These letters all start with a loop.
Start at the red dots and follow the arrows to trace them.

d d d d d 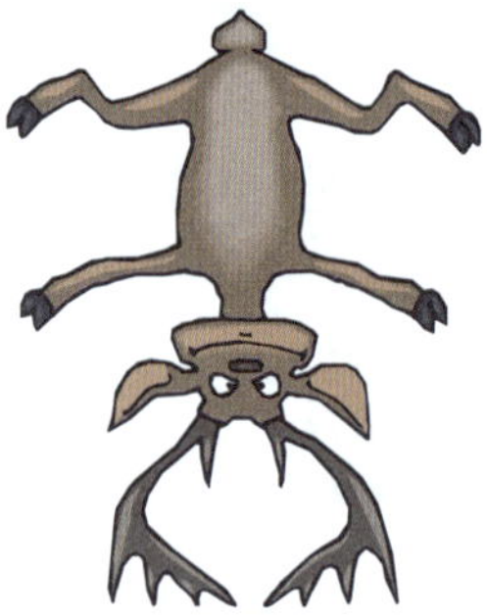 d

g 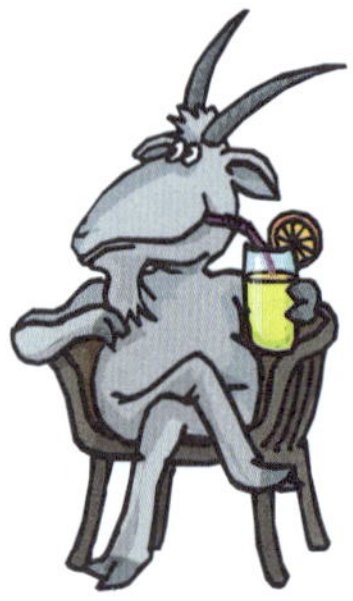 g g g g g

q q q 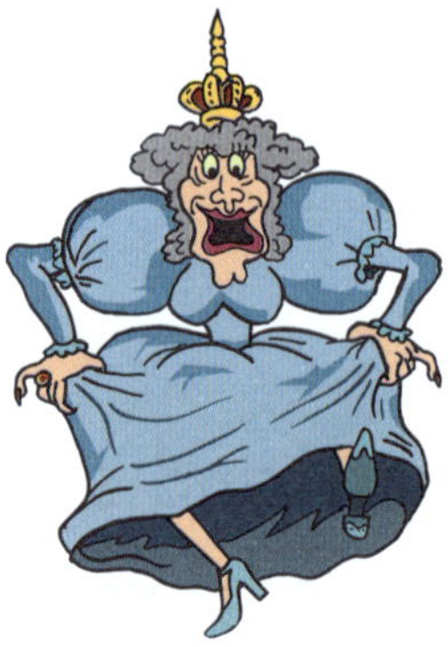 q q

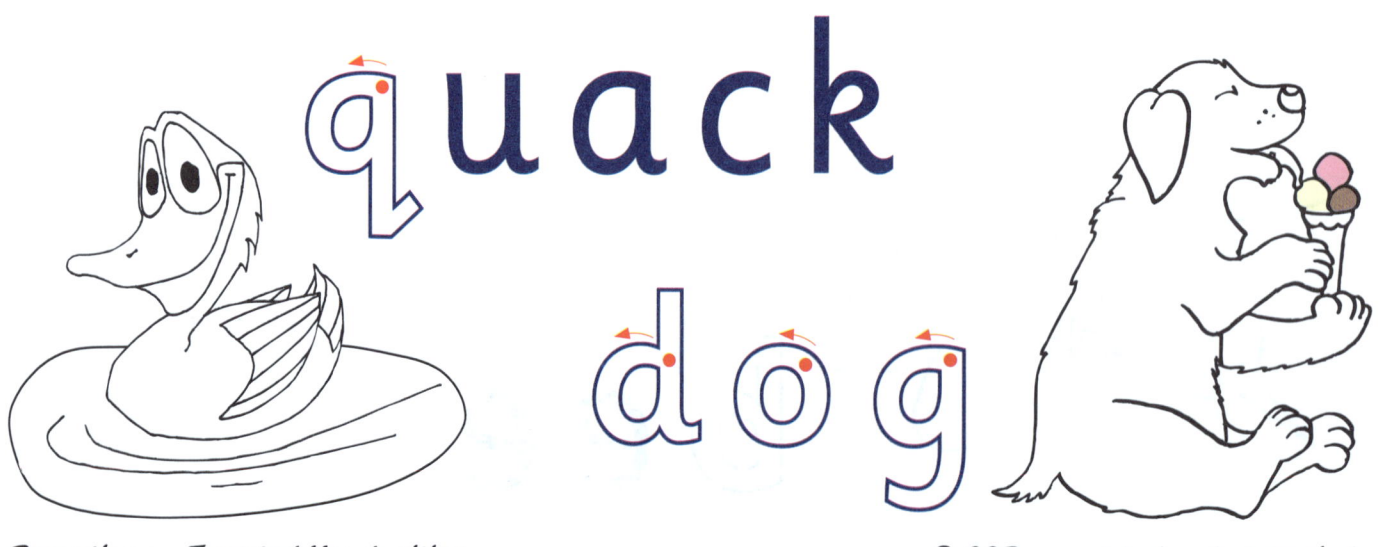

Complete the words by tracing the missing letters.
You need to stay inside the lines. Then colour in the pictures.

quack

dog

e, s and f

These three letters are all curly.
Draw over the dotty lines, starting at the red dots.

e e e 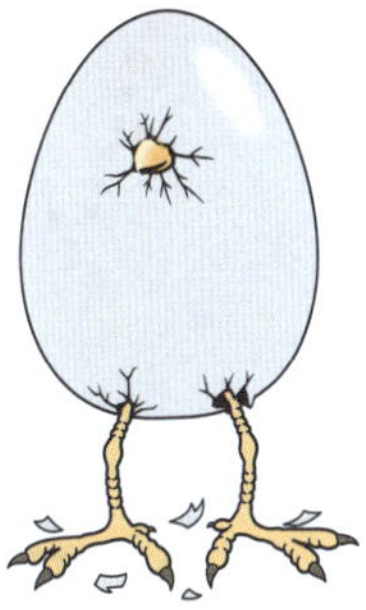 e e e

s s s s s s

f f f f f

Start at the red dots and trace these letters.
When you've finished, colour in the bear and the fish.

bear

fish

v, w, x and z

These four letters are all made up of straight lines. Start at the red dots and follow the arrows.

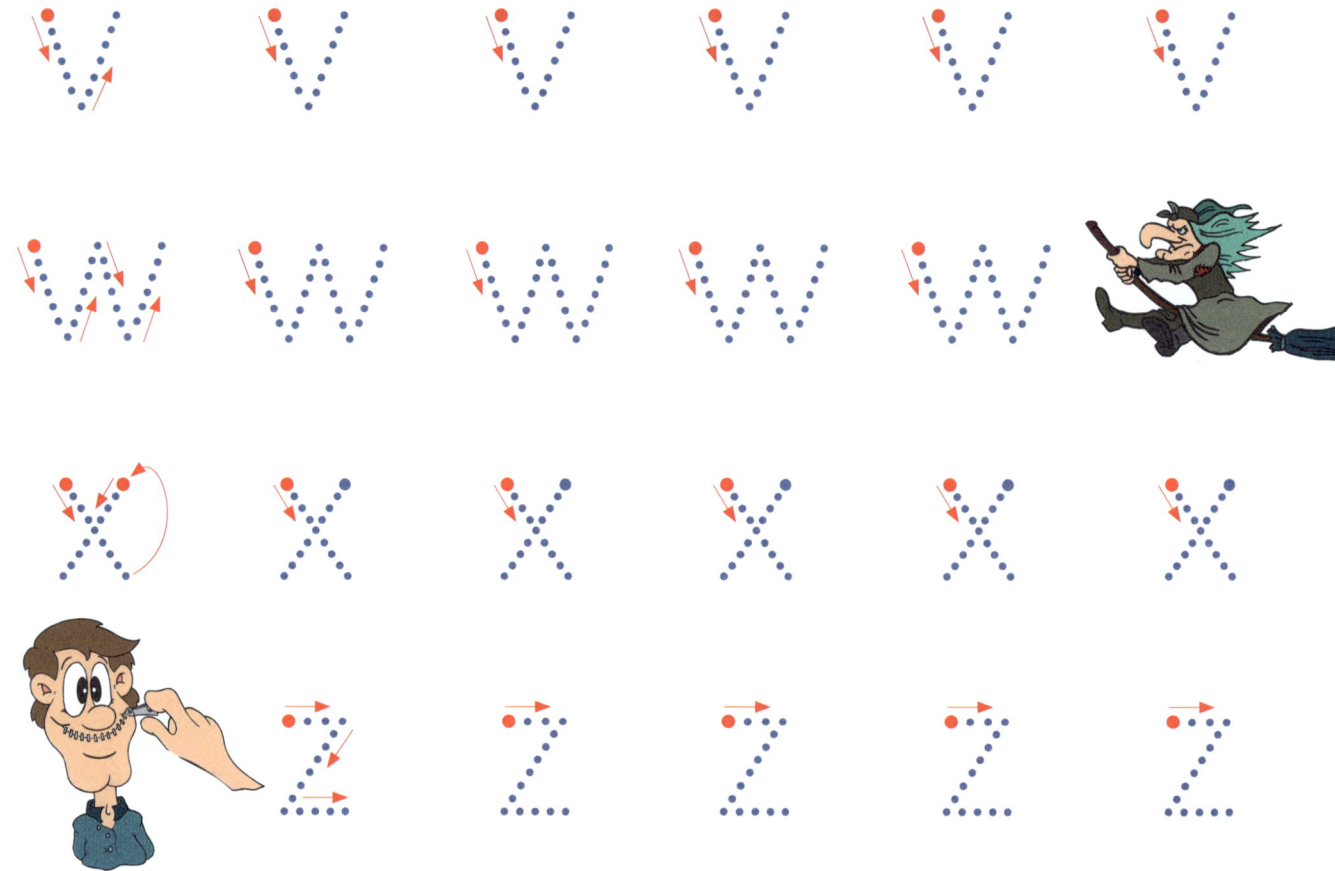

Trace these letters and make sure you stay inside the lines. Colour in the pictures once you're finished.

The Alphabet

Now it's time to go back over all the letters.
There are some pictures for you to colour in as well.

a a a a

b b b b

c c c c c c

d d d d d

e e e e

f f f f

g g g g g

h h h h h

The Alphabet

Now trace over the dots for these letters. There are three pictures to colour in on this page.

Reception — Targeted Handwriting

The Alphabet

Here's the last page of letters for you to trace.
Colour in the pictures when you're done.

r r r    s s s

t t t t

u u u u

v v v v

w w w w

x x x x

y y y y

z z z z

Numbers

Trace over the dotty lines to complete the numbers. Start at the red dots and follow the arrows.

0 0 0 0 0

1 1 1 1 1

2 2 2 2 2

3 3  3 3 3

4 4 4 4 4

Trace the number and try to stay inside the lines. Then colour in the same number of stars.

3 stars

Reception — Targeted Handwriting © CGP — not to be photocopied

Numbers

Here are some more numbers for you to trace.
Start at the red dots and draw over the dotty lines.

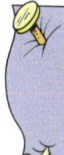

5 5 5 5 5

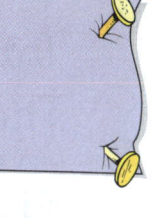

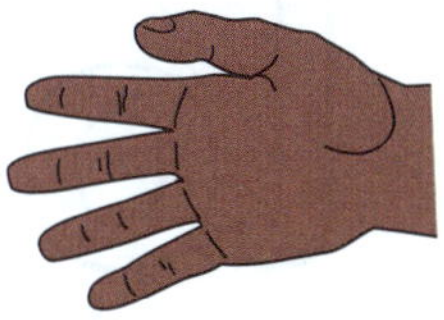

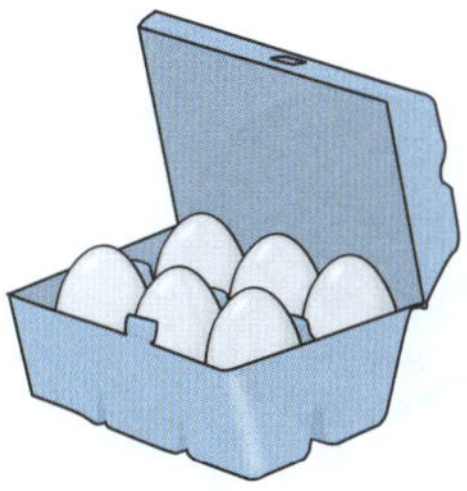

 6 6 6 6 6

7 7 7 7 7

8 8 8 8 8

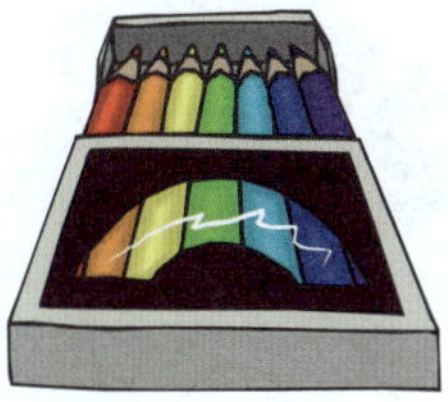

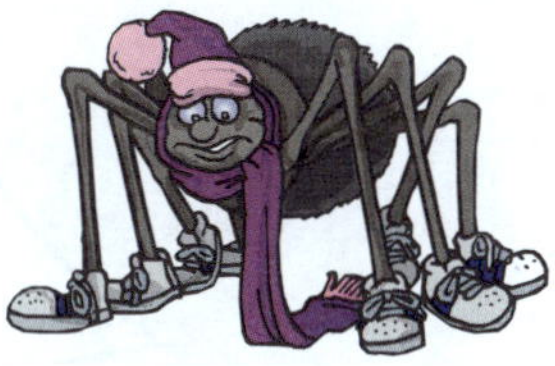

9 9 9 9 9

How many circles are there? Trace the right number.

5 6 7 8 9

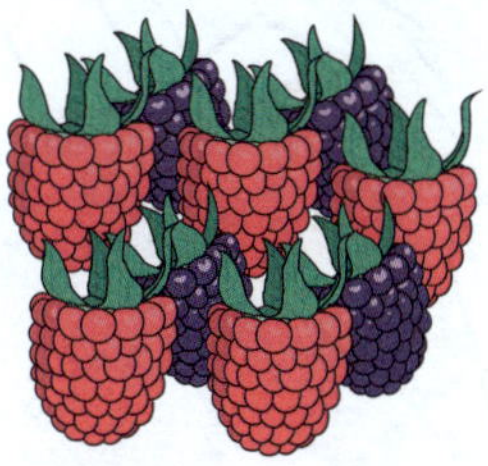

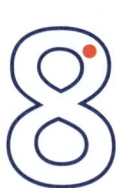

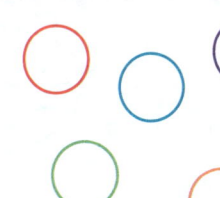

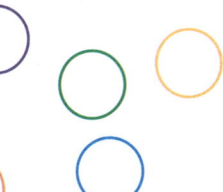

Grand Finale

Trace all the letters and the dotty lines. Then you can colour in the pictures.

lost in space

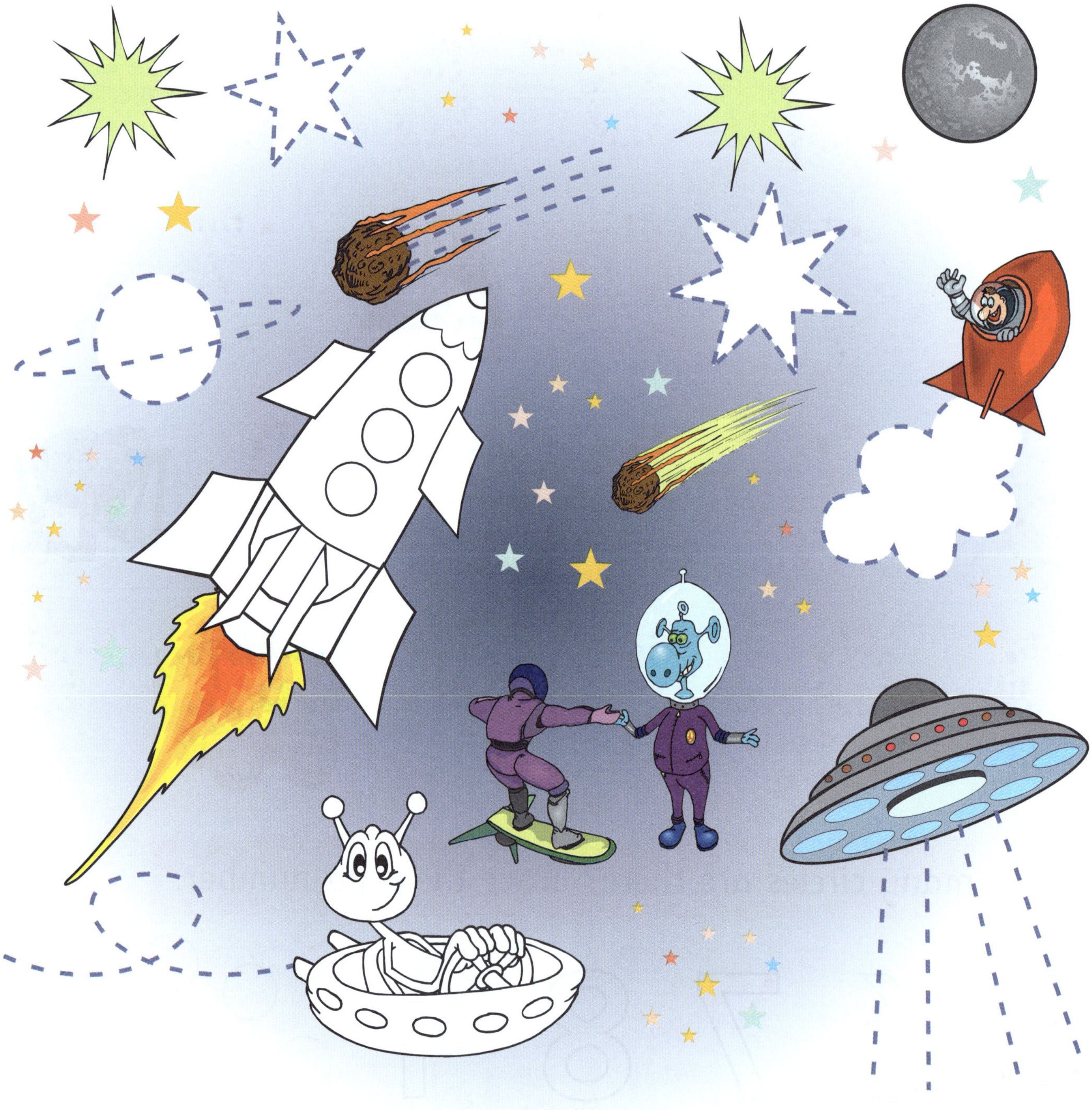